Celebrating the Family

Lessons from the Book of Ruth

Bishop Timothy J. Clarke

ISBN 978-09764022-0-6

Powerful Purpose Publishing Company
P O Box 32132 — Columbus, OH 43232

Publishing Consultant. Obieray Rogers (www.rubiopublishing.com)

Printed in the United States of America.

This work is dedicated to my sisters:
Pam, Laura, Jackie.
I love you three, and I am glad
we are family!

Table of Contents

Introduction:
The Family Is Alive and Well

There are some people who would have us believe that the family is doomed, there is no chance of resurrection, and they are ready to attend a funeral. I am not ready to pronounce, "Earth to earth, ashes to ashes, and dust to dust" on the family. The family may be sick, but like Jesus said about Lazarus, *"This sickness is not unto death"* (John 11:1-4). There is still life in the family. To paraphrase Shakespeare: "I have not come to bury the family, but to praise it" and to say that we have a future and a hope. We must learn how to celebrate the family.

For every man who deserts his family, there are millions who stay. For every welfare mother who cheats the system, there are millions who don't. For every dropout, crackhead, and murderer, there are millions of young people who are doing the right thing. The media has done a thorough job of portraying the negative images, so we are afraid to drive through certain neighborhoods or walk down certain streets, but in spite of the media, there are positive family role models.

A study of the Book of Ruth will help us discover what it means to be family — both biological and spiritual. Every family is important to God, whether it is the traditional family with father, mother, and children; a single parent family with the father or mother raising children alone; a family dealing with the hell of a divorce; a family in transition bouncing back from the loss of a spouse, or a family dealing with empty-nest syndrome. All families are important to God. The book of Ruth reinforces that God is in control regardless of the family you have.

Throughout *Celebrating the Family: Lessons from the Book of Ruth* we will discover that Elimelech, Naomi, Kilion, Orpah, Mahlon, Ruth, and Boaz were ordinary people used by God. We will also discover that they had problems, troubles, and disappointments; yet, in spite of what they went through, God was right there with them. They had struggles and trials, highs and lows, mountains and valleys, joys and sorrows. One of the things we will notice is that families are the same everywhere. If we didn't know which century the Book of Ruth was written in, we would assume it was a story set in the present.

I am convinced the reason God had me write this book is two-fold. First, the family is under attack. I don't know of an age or time when the family unit as we know it is being more severely tested than right now. Secondly, I believe God is about to begin a revival of the family. As we move closer to the Second Coming, God is going to do something in the life of both the Church and families. We need to be aware of what is happening around us. There is no doubt that families are suffering, struggling, and under siege by pressures from the outside and from the enemy as well.

The Book of Ruth is a story about ordinary people, going through ordinary problems, who served an extraordinary God. God used these ordinary people to teach us that the family is worth celebrating.

Chapter One:
A Prodigal Family

You are probably familiar with the story of the Prodigal Son told in Luke 15:11-31. The younger son said to his father, "Look, I don't want to wait until you die. Give me what's mine right now." Jesus said that the father, loving his two sons, gave to the younger the portion that would have naturally gone to him upon the father's death. The younger son took his possessions, moved to a far country, and spent all he had. The Bible says that he ended up in a pigpen not only feeding swine, but also willing to eat the husks that the pigs refused. If you have ever seen an ear of corn with all the kernels gone, then you know the only thing left is an ugly, dried-up husk. That is what this young man was willing to eat.

This is what sin will do to you. The world will not tell you that when you live in sin you end up in the pigpen. The world will only show you the glamour and glory of sin. It is on every television show, every movie, everything that is advertised. If you drink, you're cool. If you smoke, you're together. If you do this, you'll be on top of the world. The world does not show you that after you smoke all of your life, you will probably end up with cancer. The world does not tell you that after you drink, you may develop cirrhosis of the liver. The world does not tell you that after you sleep around, you could contract AIDS or another STD. The world does not tell you if you live in sin, you will end up in the pigpen. Drugs will lead you to the pigpen. Liquor will lead you to the pigpen. Sex outside of marriage will lead you to the pigpen. And living estranged from God will lead you to the pigpen.

Jesus said this young man finally came to himself and said, "I will arise and go to my father and ask him to make me a hired servant." The story is wonderful because when the young man returned home, he discovered that his father had been waiting for him all the time to return him to the position of son-ship. One of the reasons we like this story is because there is a little of the Prodigal Son in all of us because we have all strayed from the Father's house at some point.

A prodigal mindset is not just confined to an individual. A nation can be prodigal. That is what is wrong with America. We have left the foundation and principles that made us great. We do not have prayer in schools or allow spirituality in the fiber of our society. As a nation we have turned from God and we are reaping the results. When we had prayer in schools, we did not have the kind of problems we have today. Fifty years ago young people were worried about whether they would pass their arithmetic test or had a date for the prom. Fifty years later our young people are worried about whether they will live to see another day. We took prayer out and guns came in. We took prayer out and the devil came in. We took prayer out and all kinds of false teaching came in. America will never be great until we go back to the Father's house and the principles that made us great.

Both an individual and a nation can be prodigal, and the Book of Ruth shows us that an entire family can also be prodigal. Like the Prodigal Son, this family left the Father's house and ended up in the pigpen.

Elimelech and his family lived in Bethlehem, Judah. Bethlehem means "House of Bread" and

Judah means "Praise" so they lived in the "House of Bread and Praise." That is a nice place to live, but Ruth 1:1 says they left the House of Bread and Praise for Moab. God had said, *"Moab is my wash pot. Over Edom I will cast out my shoe; over Philistia I will triumph"* (Psalm 108:9, KJV), which is a polite way of calling Moab a "garbage can." Elimelech moved his family from the House of Bread and Praise to a garbage can! So what made Elimelech move his family to a garbage can and become prodigal?

FAMINE

Biblical archeology reveals that Palestine, where Bethlehem was located, had a very unpredictable rainy season. It was no surprise that there was a drought and a famine. There are only three possible causes for a famine: natural (unpredictable rain pattern), military (war), or spiritual (God's judgment). There are two causes of spiritual famine: hoarding and sin. When people decide not to share with others, it causes a famine. Consequently, when there is a famine, people will do anything to survive. When a church is going through a famine, they will attempt to manufacture the power of God. When a nation is going through a famine, they will attempt to manufacture the approval of God. When a family is going through a famine, they will try to obtain and accumulate more material possessions in the hopes of manufacturing the presence of God.

I don't think it is too far of a stretch to say that families today are going through a famine. There is a famine of morals, principles, discretion, values, importance, and love. So many families are on the brink of a famine, yet they look good on the outside. There is a famine in your life, but instead of turning to God you turn to other things. You make statements like, "I don't have time to go to church because I have to take my family to the movies today." Or "I promised my child I'd take him/her to the amusement park." Or "I haven't spent any time with my family, so this weekend we're not going to church; we're going to do something else." That is like leaving the House of Bread and Praise and going to the garbage can. What greater tool can you use to teach your family how to stop a famine than to worship God? When the famine comes, you need to connect to Someone who has the kind of food your soul needs.

FEAR

Elimelech and Naomi were from a well off family. When the famine hit Elimelech said, "I can't imagine not having everything I've always had, so I'm going to leave the House of Bread and Praise and go live in the garbage can so I can stay comfortable." He was afraid of sacrifice, self-denial, and the cost of sticking with God.

Prodigal families leave God because they can't imagine not having everything they have now. They run from God, trying to hold onto what they think gives meaning to their lives. Elimelech and his family left Bethlehem to avoid trouble and death. They went to Moab and ran smack into trouble and death. Elimelech went to Moab and died while trying to save his life from starvation. They left the House of Bread and Praise and ran to the garbage can so they would not have to suffer in the famine, but they ended up running into suffering that could have been avoided if they had stayed with God.

Some of you are running from God, but you are running smack into the very thing you are trying to run from. You are running from God because you think He is going to put you into bondage. You are going to run into something that will have you bound like you have never been bound before, because you will run right into what you are trying to escape.

If Elimelech and Naomi had just waited on God, the famine would have ended. I would rather be with God in the midst of a famine in Bethlehem than by myself in Moab with a table full of food.

FAILURE

Failure to trust God and failure to live like the people of God caused this family to become prodigal. Do you know what is making our families prodigal today? It is failure to live like we belong to God. When children go astray, parents often ask, "Where did I go wrong? I gave them everything," and I want to stop them and say, "You just answered your own question. You gave them everything." When you give a child everything, they never have to work for anything and usually will not appreciate anything. You do not make a child blessed by giving them everything. You give a child the things that matter most, and nothing is more important than introducing them to a right relationship with the God of their salvation.

Although he lived in the House of Bread and Praise and God was all around him, Elimelech failed because there was no God inside of him. A lot of people go to church, but there is no God in them because they do not live, walk, or act like they know Him. When the storms are raging, they leave God to go live in the garbage can. When you have God in you, the storms may be raging, the wind may be blowing, and the rain may be falling, but you know who you are and where you are. While the storms are raging you are telling God, "I'm not letting go. I don't believe you brought me this far to leave me."

I once heard a story about a wounded eagle that ended up in a chicken coup. The chickens treated him nice and accepted him into their fellowship. One day a man took the eagle aside and said, "Listen, you're not a chicken, you're an eagle." He took the eagle to the river so he could see his reflection in the water and said, "You see those feathers? Spread your wings. You see that wingspan? That's not a chicken span, that's an eagle span. Look at your beak. That's not a chicken beak, but an eagle's beak. Look up in the sky. You see those big birds flying so majestically? Those are eagles, and that's where you belong. Not down here clucking with the chickens, but soaring with the eagles." But the eagle said, "I've been around chickens so long I don't know if I can fly anymore. I don't know if I can get up there where the other eagles are." The man said, "Yes you can, because you've got eagle inside you. You were not made to stay on the ground. You were made to fly in the air with majesty and splendor, grace and dignity. You're not a chicken. You're an eagle." After a while the eagle began believing and started flapping his wings, flexing his muscles, shaking his head, and bopping his beak. He started running the length of the yard and took off into flight and every time he flapped his wings he said, "I'm an eagle. I can fly. I can make it!"

Like that eagle, you can stand up, spread your wings, and fly! There is some God in you. You were not made to live in the garbage can. Get up and go home. Go back to the Father and say, "I'm sorry." If you sincerely mean it, God will take you back. It does not matter what you have done or how badly you have messed up. God's grace is sufficient. He loves you and He will forgive you and cleanse you.

DYING IN THE WRONG PLACE

Elimelech left the House of Bread and Praise to live in the garbage can. I wish he had come to himself like the Prodigal Son and gone back to Bethlehem, but he died in Moab. Elimelech never got the chance to do what he should have done, which was to go back home.

DON'T DIE OUTSIDE THE WILL OF GOD

Elimelech died in Moab, but it was not just the city of his death; it was the attitude that he had in the city. It is bad enough Elimelech died in Moab geographically, but he also died in Moab spiritually. There is a fate worse than death and that is dying outside the will of God.

I don't think Elimelech intended to stay in Moab. Look at this passage:

> *Now it came to pass in the days when the judges ruled, that there was a famine in the land. And a certain man of Bethlehem Judah went to sojourn in the country of Moab, he,*

and his wife, and his two sons." (Ruth 1:1, KJV)

That word "sojourn" means a resident alien. Elimelech did not become a citizen of Moab, but he became a resident alien. One of the things a resident alien does is put himself under the protection of the ruler of the country where he presently resides. When you become a resident alien, you are saying, "I trust the ruler of this land to take care of me." Sojourn is when you go on a trip with the intention of returning back home.

Elimelech went to Moab to save his family from dying and to escape the famine. When you go to another country and put yourself under the protection of another "god," you have no control over whether you will ever get back home. This is what happens to sinners. They do not plan to die in sin, but when you go to live in Moab, there is the potential of never going home again.

Elimelech did not plan to stay in Moab. He probably said, "I'll only be here a couple of months. I'll get some money and then go back to what I know is right. I'm going to take care of business over here and go home in a few days." Yet, the days turned into weeks, the weeks into months, and the months into years. The longer he stayed in Moab, the harder it was to go back home. He probably promised Naomi that "one day" or "next year" they would go back to Bethlehem. He never made it back.

DON'T DIE WITHOUT REALIZING YOUR FULL POTENTIAL

Psychologists tell us that most people die having reached only twenty to thirty percent of their potential. Most of you can do far more than what you are doing, regardless of your age:

> *What is man that you are mindful of him, and the son of man that you visit him? For you have made him a little lower than the angels, and you have crowned him with glory and honor. You have made him to have dominion over the works of your hands; you have put all things under his feet.* (Psalm 8:4-6, NKJV)

God has made us a little lower than Himself which means we have so much potential inside. Most of us will die and never realize half of it.

Elimelech died without realizing his potential. How do I know? Because of what his name means. In Old Testament days, parents named their children based on what they saw in them and what they wanted for them. Elimelech's name means, "My God is King." He would never realize the potential of his name living in Moab. By his very geographical location he limited what he could do.

Can you imagine what a witness Elimelech was at work and in his neighborhood? Remember they didn't say Elimelech in English like we would say it today. Every time someone greeted him they said, "Hello, My God is King. How are you doing today, My God is King?"

Now can you imagine what the Moabites said when "My God is King" left the House of Bread and Praise and went to live in the garbage can? Every time Elimelech ate Moabite food and lived in the Moabite land, it was an opportunity for the enemies of God to make fun of his name. The same way he witnessed for God in Bethlehem is the same way he became a joke in Moab. Why would anybody in Moab let a man named "My God is King" do anything? His very name was an insult to them and a contradiction to everything they stood for because they worshipped all kinds of gods.

Elimelech lost his witness and gave the Moabites an opportunity to make fun of God's name. They probably wondered, "If God is king, what's he doing in Moab? Why is he eating our food, living in our land and letting his sons marry our women? If God is such a king, why isn't he taking care of and providing for his family?" Every time Elimelech walked through Moab, they laughed and said, "Look, here's My God is King. What a joke."

When you have God's name and take it to the garbage can, you drag His name down with you. That is why you cannot just go everywhere, do everything you want, and say anything you please. You have God's name and you must live like it. When you live beneath your privilege, when you talk out of both sides of your mouth, when you do not live up to what God has put inside of you and claimed for you, you give the world and the devil an opportunity to make fun of both you and the God you serve. You ought to make up your mind that you are going to stand so that no one will be able to make a mockery of your God.

Some of you are not going to be able to do what you need to do from where you are now. You are limiting your potential by your very location. You need to move to where God wants you. Why would the devil let you do anything in his land? Do you think the devil is going to make it easy for you to break from habits, people, things, and surrender to the lordship of Jesus? Do you think the devil is going to make it easy for you to break away from your friends and run to Jesus? He is going to do whatever he has to do, and use whomever he can to make it as hard as possible. You have to make up your mind that you are not dying where you are. There is a God who is able to give you the power to make your break with the devil.

There is a story told about Michelangelo who one day walked by a stone quarry and saw a block of marble. He asked the quarry master for it and the man said, "Take it. It's an odd shape and nobody wants it." Michelangelo took it home, set it down, and looked at it from various angles. He sent his assistants out of the room and worked on the marble day and night. They could hear him working, but they didn't know what he was doing and they wondered why Michelangelo was wasting time on that oddly shaped piece of marble. After working for months he finally let them see what he had been doing. He had created a piece that would become known as Michelangelo's Little David. One of his assistants asked him where the statute came from and Michelangelo responded, "It was in the marble all the time. It just needed somebody who could see it and release it."

What is in you that God sees and knows is there because He put it there? What you need to do is allow God to chisel away and work on you until what is inside comes out. The world does not see it, but God does. Do not die without realizing your potential.

DON'T DIE WITHOUT GETTING YOUR HOUSE IN ORDER

Elimelech's children, Mahlon and Kilion, were never told what it meant to be a man or a Jew because both Mahlon and Kilion married Moabite women. Jews were to keep their bloodline pure and were forbidden to marry outside of their race. Elimelech died before telling his sons what it meant to be set apart in the eyes of God.

I don't have to tell you how many of our children are growing up with a daddy who has not taught them what it means to be a man or a woman. This is why we have so many young men standing on street corners, because their daddy never taught them what it means to be made in the image and likeness of God. This is why we have young girls having babies while still babies themselves, because their daddy never taught them they were special and that what they possess is the most precious thing they have. Their daddy never told them they couldn't give themselves to any and everybody without destroying themselves in the process.

Teach your children about God. Not just in their head but in their heart. Teach them about His power and His might. Teach them about His strength and grace. Teach them about His joy and love. We must not die until we get our house in order.

Chapter Two:
Don't Give Up On Hope

There is nothing more damaging than when an individual loses hope. But what do you do when hope dies?

At the end of chapter one, Naomi is getting ready to say goodbye to Ruth and Orpah. These three women had more than their share of trouble and grief. Now comes the time when they must leave each other. It is a tender moment. Anyone who has ever had to leave home or move away from friends and loved ones knows the pain these women were feeling. Tender ties may have bound them, but reality was pulling them apart.

Ruth and Orpah wanted to stay with Naomi, but Naomi told them the truth: There would be no more sons. She had no family in Moab; and if they went back to Bethlehem with her, they would, in essence, forfeit or give up their entire futures. It is a bleak picture; yet, we all may have faced moments like this. At those times it seems like hope is gone.

There is nothing sadder than the death of hope. When you have lost everything else, you can hold on for a better tomorrow if you have hope.

What do you do when hope dies? That was Naomi's question and it is ours, as well. What do you do when the marriage is over? What do you do when the flames of love have burned out? What do you do when the prognosis is cancer and the doctor says, "It has spread too far to stop?" What do you do when dreams seem further and further away and goals seem unreachable? That was Naomi's dilemma. If we are honest, we have been there, too. We tried, but hope was gone. It had died and we are left in Moab for the funeral. I believe there are three things that contribute to the death of hope. Perhaps if we can recognize what contributes to the death of hope, we can prevent it and keep hope alive.

HOPE DIES WHEN WE RELY ON OUR OWN RESOURCES

But Naomi said, "Return home my daughters. Why would you come with me? Am I going to have more sons who could become your husbands? Return home, my daughters; I am too old to have another husband. Even if

I thought there was still hope for me — even if I had a husband tonight and then gave birth to sons — would you wait until they grew up? Would you remain unmarried for them? No, my daughters. It is more bitter for me than for you, because the Lord's hand has gone out against me!" (Ruth 1:11-13(a))

Do you notice how many times Naomi refers to "me," "my," and "I"? She is obsessed with herself and that is the beginning of the end of hope. Whenever all you see is what you have, or don't have, and rely on your own resources, it will not be long before what you have runs out. When you are consumed with what you have, or don't have, you are destined to become discouraged because there is always somebody with more than you. Stop comparing yourself to other people. You do not know what they have gone through, or what they are going through, to have what they have. When you walk around comparing yourself to others, you snuff out hope. Thank God for whatever you have because He has given you what you need. When you dwell only on what you have, and rely only on your own resources, hope dies because sooner or later, you are going to run out.

25

Timothy J. Clarke

Remember the feeding of the five thousand?

*After this, Jesus crossed over to the far side of
the Sea of Galilee, also known as the Sea of
Tiberias. A huge crowd kept following him
wherever he went, because they saw his mira-
culous signs as he healed the sick. Then Jesus
climbed a hill and sat down with his disciples
around him. (It was nearly time for the Jewish Passover celebration.) Jesus soon saw a
huge crowd of people coming to look for him.
Turning to Philip, he asked, "Where can we
buy bread to feed all these people?" He was
testing Philip, for he already knew what he
was going to do. Philip replied, "Even if we
worked for months, we wouldn't have enough
money to feed them!" Then Andrew, Simon
Peter's brother, spoke up. "There's a young
boy here with five barley loaves and two fish.
But what good is that with this huge
crowd?" "Tell everyone to sit down," Jesus
said. So they all sat down on the grassy
slopes. (The men alone numbered about
5,000). Then Jesus took the loaves, gave
thanks to God, and distributed them to the*

people. Afterward he did the same with the fish. And they all ate as much as they wanted. After everyone was full, Jesus told his disciples, "Now gather the leftovers, so that nothing is wasted." So they picked up the pieces and filled twelve baskets with scraps left by the people who had eaten from the five barley loaves. (John 6:1-13, NLT)

Remember the man of God who was surrounded by the enemy?

When the servant of the man of God got up early the next morning and went outside, there were troops, horses, and chariots everywhere. "Oh, sir, what will we do now?" the young man cried to Elisha. "Don't be afraid!" Elisha told him. "For there are more on our side than on theirs!" Then Elisha prayed, "O LORD, open his eyes and let him see!" The LORD opened the young man's eyes, and when he looked up, he saw that the hillside around Elisha was filled with horses and chariots of fire. (2 Kings 6:15-17, NLT)

The point of these two passages is to remind you not to rely on your own resources. You may be at the end of your rope, but there are invisible resources available to give you what you need when you don't feel like you have anything left.

HOPE DIES WHEN WE DWELL ONLY ON THE NEGATIVE

"It is more bitter for me than for you, because the Lord's hand has gone out against me!" (Ruth 1:13(b)). Naomi forgot that she was in Moab by her own choosing. Nowhere in the Book of Ruth do we read where Naomi tried to talk Elimelech out of leaving Bethlehem. She went willingly to Moab, settled there, and allowed their sons to marry Moabite women. When trouble came, she got mad at God because Moab had turned into a wilderness. She had a lot of nerve. She didn't pray about what she did and then wanted to blame God. Naomi also forgot that in spite of all that had happened, she was still alive. Elimelech, Mahlon, and Kilion were all dead.

Some of you are the same way. No one told you to get married, but you did. We asked you not to, but you just had to have him or her. No one told you to leave home, but you wanted to be your own boss and do your own thing. You thought you could have everything your way. Don't get mad at God when your plans become messed up. The next time you want to have a pity party, remember it may be bad but at least you are still alive. Your spouse may have left, but you are still alive. You may have gotten laid off, but you are still alive. You may not have all you want, but you are still alive. And as long as there is life, there is hope.

Nothing we have — marriage, job, school, family, or life — will be successful if we only focus on the negative. Focusing only on the negative will drain you. Do you know why you are ready to spiritually and emotionally cut your throat and slit your wrist? Hope died. And what killed it was that you only focused on the negatives.

HOPE DIES WHEN WE LEAVE
GOD OUT OF THE EQUATION

According to Jewish law, if a man died, the next of kin was to marry the wife and raise the firstborn from that union as if he were the child of the deceased husband (Deuteronomy 25:5-9). That is called the kinsman redeemer. Naomi told her daughters-in-law that there were no more sons in her so they might as well stay in Moab while she returned to Bethlehem. That is where she messed up. She left God out of the equation.

When you get to the end of the Book of Ruth, you will discover that God did, in fact, have a kinsman redeemer already in place. He didn't have to be born and they didn't have to wait for him to grow up. Boaz was a relative on Elimelech's side, which meant there was no bloodline between him and Naomi. Actually, the Hebrew translation for family used in this text refers to a close friend, so there may not have been a bloodline between Boaz and Elimelech at all, just friendship. Although the inference is that Boaz may not have been blood, he was family just the same, and he stepped up to help Naomi.

There are some women who think that both the Bible and God are sexist and that it only speaks about men, which is not true. There is no book in the world that elevates women to a higher place than the Bible. There is no person or being in the world that has more respect for women than God. When God created the concept of the kinsman redeemer,

He didn't do it to make women feel inferior, but to protect their virtue. If a woman's husband died and there were no children, she was left to raise cattle, tend the farm, and harvest the grain all by herself. Can you imagine a woman behind a yoke of oxen? Can you imagine a woman digging in the field, planting the field, harvesting the grain with no help at all? If a woman was left without offspring after her husband died, God said that somebody had to help take care of her.

We live in a day and time when women want to pretend they don't need help, but there are some things a woman should not do. That does not make you less than or inferior to a man; it means that God has made women different and special. One of the worst things that can happen is for a woman to step out of her place and start acting like a man.

When God instituted the concept of the kinsman redeemer, He was seeking to secure the place of women in society. Israel in the Old Testament was far different from America in the twenty-first century. Women were not seen as equal and were less valuable than cattle. They were objects to be used and abused. God sought to establish and preserve the virtue, glory, and honor of women. In those days a widow had two options: wife or prostitute. She could not go to corporate Jerusalem and get a job as a CEO. Her place was in the home; and if she didn't have one, it was the streets. As a way to protect her, God instituted the kinsman redeemer.

Jerusalem held the answer to her dilemma, but Naomi couldn't see it because she left God out of the equation. She was counting on herself and a man, and what she needed was going to take more than a man. It was going to take God.

God has to be part of any successful equation. Situations are bound to look hopeless when He is left out. When God is in the mix, what seems impossible all of a sudden becomes possible because God specializes in things that seem impossible.

KEEP HOPE ALIVE

George Frederick Watts created a painting of a solitary figure sitting on top of planet earth with a one-string harp. The painting is called *Hope*. When asked why he named it *Hope*, Mr. Watts said, "Because hope will play when everything else looks bad. Even when all the harp strings are broken, hope keeps on playing."

You may only have one string left, but hope says keep on playing even when you feel like giving up. Hope says it is not over yet because there is still life in you, and by the grace of God you can make it.

Chapter Three:
Saying Goodbye

"Intreat me not to leave thee," begins one of the most familiar and beloved passages from the Book of Ruth:

> *And Ruth said, Intreat me not to leave thee, or to return from following after thee: for whither thou goest, I will go; and where thou lodgest, I will lodge: thy people shall be my people, and thy God my God: Where thou diest, will I die, and there will I be buried: the LORD do so to me, and more also, if ought but death part thee and me.* (Ruth 1:16-17, KJV)

All of us want to know the kind of love expressed by Ruth to Naomi. These words demonstrate the bond that should exist between all of us, and especially those of us who are members of the family of God. Can we be honest? We hear a lot about love, sing about love, and talk about love, but if there is one thing lacking in this world, it is real and genuine love. There is no end to the love songs on the radio. There is no end to those who tell us how much they love us. But, when you really get down to it, what the world is looking for is a genuine expression of love. Matter of fact, if you ask most people what they want out of a relationship, they would tell you, "I just want to know that I am loved."

For all our familiarity with this passage, we do not realize there is a story behind the story. Naomi had made the decision to leave Moab and encouraged her daughters-in-law (Ruth and Orpah) to return to their families. Although Ruth and Orpah were Moabites, Naomi was considered the matriarch of the family and had the responsibility for their care. When the husband and the sons died and there were no other men in the family, Naomi became the responsible person, and all of the authority that Elimelech, Mahlon, and Kilion had was transferred to Naomi upon their deaths. Was that God's plan? No. Was that God's perfect will? No. But God will use whoever is available to get the job done.

Although Bethlehem was not their home, Ruth and Orpah were bound by custom to follow Naomi. Keep that in mind because it has bearing on the story. Here were three women alone in the world, starting on a journey without knowing what the end would be.

> *"Return home, my daughters. Why would you come with me? Am I going to have any more sons who could become your husbands? Return home, my daughters; I am too old to have another husband. Even if I thought there was still hope for me – even if I had a husband tonight and then gave birth to sons – would you wait until they grew up? Would you remain unmarried for them?"*
> (Ruth 1:11-13(a))

There is a point in this story we often miss. Preachers use this text and focus on Ruth and her love for Naomi and by doing so we unconsciously make Orpah the ungrateful, selfish, and disobedient one who was only looking out for herself. What I want to suggest is that if we take another look at Orpah, we will discover she is not as bad as we have always made her out to be.

If you were to ask who was the better daughter-in-law Ruth would win hands down because she stuck with Naomi. However, if you look at the text,

37

you will discover that Orpah was the obedient one. Naomi gave them both a command: *"Go back home. Each of you return to your mother's house"* (Ruth 1:8). Who obeyed? Orpah. Who disobeyed? Ruth. Who was right? They both were. This is one text where there is virtue in obedience and disobedience.

The assumption is that Orpah left Naomi and went back to the good life, but that is wrong. She had married young, had depended on her husband to take care of her, and her father before marriage. By custom it was Naomi's job to look after her once she became a widow and it appeared that Naomi was trying to renege on her responsibility. It seemed like Naomi was saying, "Look, I don't know how to take care of myself, let alone you. Go home. Fend for yourself." Orpah went from her daddy's house to her husband's. She never held a job, never knew how to balance a checkbook. Orpah's husband was dead and her mother-in-law said, "Go home." But what was she going home to? Uncertainty? Lack of security? She didn't know. She never had to fend for herself, but all of a sudden she had to go home and be responsible for the rest of her life. Orpah was a Moabite who married a Jew. What Moabite man wanted a woman who had married outside her race? Before we judge Orpah too harshly, we need to walk in her shoes. When she said goodbye to Naomi, she was saying goodbye to all the security she had ever known.

Then look at Ruth. She was willing to leave family and friends to follow Naomi. Saying goodbye for her also meant leaving everything she knew in Moab.

And what about Naomi? When she said goodbye, she left the remains of three people she loved most in the world in Moab. How do you think she felt saying goodbye?

SAYING GOODBYE
MEANS HAVING TO LET GO

There is a difference between letting go and giving up. We may never give up, but we all have to learn how to let go, and that is one of the hardest things to do. Some of you have stayed in relationships that are unhealthy and destructive because you don't want to let go. Some have stayed in domestic violence situations, or relationships that are mentally and emotionally unhealthy. You keep thinking you can fix it, you can make it right, you can change him or her, but the bottom line is the only reason you are still there is because you don't want to say goodbye. Saying goodbye means you have to let go and you don't want to do that. So you stay and you die a little bit every day because you do not know how to let go. Some of you have habits that are killing you, and you cannot let go. Friends who are pulling you down surround some of you, and you cannot let go. We indulge habits, go through guilt, and stay in bondage because we do not want to let go. How many of you are living hampered and crippled lives, letting your past hinder you, because you cannot let go of something or someone?

For Naomi, saying goodbye meant leaving the memories of Elimelech, Mahlon, and Kilion. How does a mother feel when she leaves the graves of her two sons? How does a wife feel when she leaves the grave of her husband? For Ruth, it meant letting go of family and friends. For Orpah, it meant letting go of the security she had come to know.

You don't know how to let go of people, places, or memories, but if you are going to have victory, you are going to have to learn. You are never going to be healed or whole until you learn how to let go. It is not about giving up; it is about letting go. If you take your hands off and turn things over to God, He will work it out. There are some things that only God can do.

SAYING GOODBYE
MEANS WALKING BY FAITH

For Naomi, Ruth, and Orpah, the tearful farewell on the road outside of Moab was the start of a new beginning. None of them knew what the future held. For Naomi and Ruth, it was a long, unprotected trip ahead. They were two women walking through hostile and dangerous territory. There was the possibility of rape, kidnap, and murder. And what would happen once they reached their destination? For Orpah, it was uncertainty of the worst kind. Would she be an outcast in her own home? Would her daddy say, "I told you not to marry that Jew. Serves you right!" Would the other Moabites say mean and nasty things to her? What would happen to her when she went home?

We don't like to say goodbye because it means walking by faith. That is why some of us have not left where we are; it is why we are dying by degrees and wasting away every day. We don't

41

know what tomorrow holds, so we would rather stay in the mess we know than to trust God to make a way. God is in control and nothing can happen that He doesn't permit or allow. He will bring you through with victory.

You may not see everything God is doing, but you must know that God is doing something. You may not understand everywhere He leads, but you know He has a road map that will not get you lost. God must know where you are going because everywhere you go, He has already been there! You must walk by faith, even though you cannot see, feel, or comprehend what God is doing.

SAYING GOODBYE
MEANS STARTING OVER

The fact of the matter is that when you say goodbye, your next word is hello. You are finishing a chapter, but not the book. The spouse who left you is just a chapter. The job you lost is just a chapter. The heartache you have is just a chapter. That disappointment you experienced is just a chapter. You may have failed or fallen, but it is only a chapter. The book is not finished.

You have to start over. That is why we do not like to say goodbye because we are comfortable with the familiar and grown accustomed to what we have always had. Saying hello means something new, something you have never experienced, and going to a place you have never been.

Starting over is never easy. It is frightening and unsettling. There are new people and new places and none of the familiar to fall back on. You cannot start over until you say goodbye. So what do you need to say goodbye to? Do you need to say, "I am through with this drama! I am writing the end of the chapter and closing the book on this. There is still life and potential in me, and I have more chapters to write."

It is time to leave. Pack your bags, throw your shoulders back, hold your head u, and wave goodbye. God is with you and He will never leave you. It may hurt to say goodbye, but sometimes you have to do it. And when you do, the next word you hear will be hello.

Chapter Four:
Welcome Home!

There are few words in the English language that are sweeter than the small, simple word "home." If you have ever had to be away from home, you know that the longer you are away, the more you miss it. The tragedy is that most of us don't appreciate home until we have left it. We leave because it is too restrictive or too confining or we believe we are being kept from enjoying life. But once you get away from home, you learn how to appreciate home. It may be in a lonely college dorm, an isolated army barrack, or a damp prison cell, but one day you will look up and say, "I sure wish I was home."

How sad it is that most people do not appreciate home until they have lost it. Many a child has left home sick of their parents' rules only to discover that life is hard and the world is cruel. Many a man has picked up and left wife and child for the glamour of a fast life only to discover that sin is costly. Many a woman has walked away from home and responsibilities only to discover that sin takes you further than you want to go and charges you more than you want to pay. We look up from the ash heap of life and wonder, "Will I ever get back home?"

Some people have left home without physically leaving by emotionally checking out. One of the greatest tragedies of many relationships, marriages, and families is that often spouses, family members, or friends have learned how to pretend that all is well when in reality all is about to blow up. One of the signs that this has taken place is that people shut down; they stop communicating and even worse, stop trying. It many ways, they stop fighting. I don't mean fighting *with* one another, but fighting *for* one another; fighting for the marriage, fighting for the family, fighting for the relationship. They give up, give in, and give over. While physically still there they have, in every meaningful way, checked out.

It was imperative that Naomi and Ruth arrive in Bethlehem at the beginning of the barley harvest. They came home at the right time. It is not enough to know what to do; we also need to know when to do it. When you do the right thing at the wrong time, you will still make a mess. Arriving in Bethlehem at the beginning of the barley harvest was not just a good time; it was the right time for Naomi and Ruth.

Naomi and Ruth suggest to us that there is a right time to move. It is one thing to look at your watch and tell what time it is; it is another to look at your life and tell what time it is. If you don't know what time it is, you are liable to move at the wrong time. And if you move at the wrong time, not only will you miss your blessing, but if you aren't careful you may find yourself outside the will of God.

Naomi and Ruth returned to Bethlehem at the beginning of the barley harvest. So what is so important about that? I'm glad you asked.

THE BARLEY HARVEST
REPRESENTED A NEW BEGINNING

The barley harvest was the first harvest of the year after the winter season and it was a time of celebration. You may wonder what that has to do with Naomi and Ruth, so I will tell you. God let them arrive in Bethlehem at the beginning of a new season and in the midst of a celebration. Why? Because these were grief-stricken women who wanted to throw a pity party and God brought them home when people were celebrating. Whenever you have gone through a dark period in life — the loss of a loved one, sickness, and setback — the tendency is to hold onto your grief and sorrow. God knows that if you hold on too long it will consume and destroy you, so He navigates your life to a place where people are rejoicing and celebrating. And in the midst of the celebration, you begin to realize how much you have to be thankful for in spite of what you are going through.

Naomi and Ruth weren't in a party mood but God said, "Enough is enough. Get on with your life. It's time to celebrate!" Grieving is healthy and we must allow people space and time to grieve. However, we must also be able to stop the grieving and begin living. That is what God did for Naomi and Ruth. He brought them home in the midst of a celebration to remind them there is life beyond problems. Naomi and Ruth were ministered to in the midst of the celebration. The barley harvest was a time of new beginning, and sometimes God lets us come home to start all over again.

THE BARLEY HARVEST
REPRESENTED A MEANS OF WITNESSING

Naomi and Ruth came home at the beginning of the barley harvest. They came from Moab, the place that represented separation, pain, and death. The first sight Ruth had of Bethlehem was when she arrived at the barley harvest. Get a picture of this in your mind. The fields were full of barley and Ruth's first glimpse is of God's people dwelling in a place that looked better than the one she left. Can you imagine coming out of the dark into the light? Can you imagine leaving famine and coming into harvest? Can you imagine leaving sin and coming into salvation? What a wondrous change and difference there is when you step into the will of God.

Ruth had lived in Moab all of her life, and Moab had taken everything she had ever loved. When she came to Bethlehem, the House of Bread and Praise, the first thing she saw were fields full of wheat and barley and plenty in the midst of famine.

Naomi and Ruth came home at the beginning of the barley harvest and God used that time to witness to Ruth, as if to say, "See what you have been missing? See what you could have? See how I

49

take care of My people?" That is why Christians should look and dress their best. Not because we are stuck up, but because everywhere we go, we represent Christ. We should be able to say to the world, "I don't have to sell drugs or my body. Look at me. Don't I look all right? God gives me everything I need." Our lives are a witness. When we are in a place where God blesses, our blessing becomes a means of witness.

THE BARLEY HARVEST REPRESENTED A REMINDER OF HOME

For Naomi, they could not have come home at a better time. The fields were full of ripened barley and it reminded her of where home really was. Home was not Moab. It was not the desert or some strange and foreign land. Home was Bethlehem, the land of God, among the people of God. Naomi discovered that although you can leave home, it is never really out of you.

Naomi was never fully content in Moab. How could she be happy in Moab after she had lived in Bethlehem? She could not and neither can we. That is why I don't worry about people who leave the

Church and the Lord. If they were ever saved, if they had ever known the joy of salvation, if they had ever known the power of the Holy Ghost, the thrill of worship and being in the presence of God, they may go out in the world for a while, but they will never have peace, rest, or satisfaction until they come home.

Remember the Prodigal Son? That boy left home, squandered all he had, and ended up in a pigpen, but he finally came to his senses and returned home. He discovered that his father had been waiting for him all the time.

You can never be at home in the world if you have ever lived in the Kingdom. When you come to your senses and decide to go back home, you will discover that not only is the Father watching for your return, but that He is waiting with open arms to say, "Come on back home. You are still my child."

HINDRANCES TO COMING HOME

Naomi had been gone a long time, but she was able to make it back home. I asked myself two questions about that: Why did it take her so long to get back home? And what would have happened if she had not gone back home? The more I tossed those questions around in my mind, the more it occurred to me that one of the reasons people do not go home is because there are hindrances to heading home. They let something or someone prevent them from getting there. Home is too important to not go back. I asked myself what could have kept Naomi from coming home and arrived at three possible scenarios.

OUR PAIN

"Don't call me Naomi," she told them. "Call me Mara, because the Almighty has made my life very bitter" (Ruth 1:20). This Scripture gives us a glimpse of the pain Naomi was going through. She was saying, "Life has been hard and painful and I don't want to go by the name God gave me. Call me Mara." That one statement lets us know that there was still pain in her life.

All of us experience pain. Pain is real and it does not matter whether it is emotional, physical, or spiritual. Everybody does not hurt the same way, but everybody hurts. Naomi said, *"Call me Mara."* What I noticed was that none of the people who heard that said, "Don't talk like that. You should know better, you're saved." They let her express her pain. A lot of us believe that since we are saved we are never supposed to admit our weaknesses. We walk about with our holier-than-thou face on, a Bible in our hand and a cross around our neck wanting people to believe that nothing affects us. We are still human and sometimes life hurts. One of the worst things you can do is deny pain. Suppressed pain is denied pain. It does not go away, it is just covered up. That is why people can just snap; one minute they are normal and the next they have gone off the deep end.

Naomi confessed her pain and the people around her allowed her that privilege. They let her talk, and sometimes we need to do the same thing. Was God against Naomi? No. Was God unfair to Naomi? No. Did she feel that way? Yes.

A lot of people will not come home because of pain. They have been hurt and are holding onto the pain, but all pain is not bad. Some pain is necessary because it facilitates healing. There is only the presence of pain when there is the presence of life. Rejoice in the hurt because the presence of pain means there is life somewhere. If you are hurting today, give God praise because as long as there is life, there is hope and the potential for healing.

OUR PAST

"I went away full. . ." (Ruth 1:21(a)). Those words from Naomi's lips give us a glimpse of her life before Moab, death, and sorrow. She was a young woman full of life, years, dreams, hopes, and plans. She was full of potential.

That is why some backsliders never come back home. They are still looking at their past and saying, "I left God full. I sang in the choir. I served on the Usher Board. I was a Trustee. I was involved. I went out full." They will never get to where God wants them by always looking at their past.

Some of you are ashamed to come back because you left God with a lot of energy and potential, and now you are older and have slowed down. Don't let your past hinder you from coming home: *"Turn, O backsliding children, saith the LORD; for I am married unto you"* (Jeremiah 3:14(a), KJV). God has not forgotten you or given up on you. If you are willing to come home, He will open the door and take you back.

OUR PRESENT PREDICAMENT

"I went away full, but the Lord has brought me back empty" (Ruth 1:21). These are very sad words. It is hard enough to come home, but to come home with nothing to show for all the time you have been gone is humiliating. That is why some people don't come home. They have nothing to show for all the years they were in sin. They did things they never thought they would. When they left home they said to themselves, "I'm only going to be out here for a little while. Just long enough to have some fun and see how the other half lives. As soon as I've had a good time, I'll come back." But you got out there and the devil got a hold of you. Now you are old and not even sure that God wants you back. If you are still alive, God wants you. One door may have closed, but He can open another. It doesn't matter how far you have strayed or how low you have stooped, you can always come home again.

I can imagine Naomi saying, "How can I go home? I left with a husband and two sons. I left as a young woman and now I'm old. I left with plenty of potential and now my best years are behind me.

How can I come back?" When you come to yourself, you will discover the Father's love is not predicated on what you have done or where you have been. He loves you! Naomi discovered she could go home in spite of her past, her pain, and her predicament.

Naomi and Ruth came home at the beginning of the barley harvest. They didn't know what was going to happen to them or how they were going to make it. But they were home; and be it ever so humble, there is still no place like it.

They arrived home at the right time. The barley harvest was a new beginning, a witness, and a reminder of home. If they had come one month earlier, the fields would still have been barren. If they had come one month later, the crop would have been harvested. They came at the beginning of the barley harvest when the people were celebrating so their sorrow could be compensated with joy. They came at the beginning of the barley harvest so Ruth could see how good it is to serve the Lord. They came at the beginning of the barley harvest to remind Naomi you can come home again.

Chapter Five:
Let's Celebrate the Family

If I were to paraphrase Ruth 2:1, I would say, "When it looked like everything had gone wrong and there was no hope or help, God brought family into Naomi's life." You might be able to identify with her. When it looked like you were down and out, God brought someone to embrace, encourage, and help you.

THE ORIGIN OF THE FAMILY

In order to understand the value of the family there must be appreciation for the first cause and effect, how and why the family came into existence. To discover that, you have to go to the Garden of Eden:

> *God formed the man from the dust of the ground and breathed into his nostrils the breath of life, and the man became a living being.* (Genesis 2:7)

Then God saw man by himself and said, "This is not good" and created woman. This means that no matter how politically correct we want to be, two men or two women living together is not a family or a marriage. We do not hate or mistreat those who have embraced the homosexual lifestyle, but it is wrong — biologically, physiologically, and morally — and the reason it is wrong is that when God made Adam and Eve, He said, *"Be fruitful and increase in number"* (Genesis 1:28). No matter how many encounters two men or two women have together they cannot be fruitful and increase in number. They are going against God's plan and will. God made man and woman and put them together.

This inclusive lifestyle that says anything is right; this genetic experimentation and implanting of seeds, this letting two gay men hook up with two lesbians to produce a baby is demonic and satanic. It is hard enough living in this crazy world without growing up looking at your daddy and daddy and your mommy and mommy. We have to learn how to be loving, yet firm. This nation is being destroyed by our failure to take a stand on issues that are morally right.

The family has its roots in the heart of God. The origin of the family is in Genesis when God made man in His image and likeness, and then made woman from the side of man.

THE PURPOSE OF THE FAMILY

Dr. Myles Munroe says that "The purpose of a thing is found in the mind of its creator." The creator of the family is God. What did God have in mind when He thought of the family?

COMPATIBILITY

God looked at Adam running through the Garden by himself and said, "This will never do." All the animals had companions and Adam was alone. *"The Lord God said, "It is not good for the man to be alone. I will make a helper suitable for him"* (Genesis 2:18). If you skip down to Genesis 2:20 the Bible says, *"So the man gave names to all the livestock, the birds of the air and all the beasts of the field. But for Adam no suitable helper was found."*

God said that none of the animals were right for Adam, so in His goodness, wisdom, and kindness, He performed surgery. God cut Adam open, reached inside, pulled out a rib, called for needle and thread, and sewed him back up. He took the chisel of His own will and on the blueprint of His own majestic mind created a woman. He shaped her at the shoulders, put a little curve at the waistline, played out the hips, tapered the thighs, and did the calves just right. Then God blew on her, woke Adam and he said, "Wo-man!" And God said, "This is compatible!"

ACCOUNTABILITY

Adam said, *"This is now bone of my bone, flesh of my flesh. She shall be called woman because she was taken out of man"* (Genesis 2:24). Within the framework of the family is both compatibility and accountability. We are not free to do what we want and have our own way. We are accountable to one another.

TRANSPARENCY

"The man and his wife were both naked, and they felt no shame" (Genesis 2:25). The family is an environment where truth and open sharing can take place. There

is free and total acceptance. That is not just for the adults; remember the charge to Adam and Eve was to be fruitful and multiply. God wanted children brought into a unit of compatibility, accountability, and transparency.

THE RESPONSIBILITY OF THE FAMILY

Belonging to a biological or spiritual family requires certain responsibilities. The family is healthy when we all do our part.

WE ARE TO OWN THE FAMILY

By that I mean we don't have the right to disown family members no matter how many times they mess up or how embarrassed we become by them. Our responsibility is to forgive them and love them. As members of the family, we must learn how to own one another. When people are down, that's when they need you the most. This is not only true in our biological family, but our spiritual family as well.

WE ARE TO PROVIDE FOR THE FAMILY

Provision is not only materialistic, but we are to love, forgive, and accept family and offer refuge and shelter. The responsibility of the family is to provide, especially for our children, an atmosphere where they feel comfortable and at home.

WE ARE TO PROTECT THE FAMILY

We live in a mean and cruel world, and we need families that protect us from the negative criticism and predictions of failure. Our children need to be protected from fear and shame. The family must be the first guard in providing that protection.

It is the women's job to protect the men and the men's job to protect the women. When people want to say bad things about us, someone needs to say, "That's not true. There are good men and women still around. Matter of fact, I'm married to one. Matter of fact, I'm raising one. Matter of fact, I'm related to one." Don't let negative comments go unchallenged, whether they are toward adults or children.

YOU ARE NOT ALONE

You may be thinking, "I don't have any family. My parents are dead and I'm an only child. I moved to this city and I don't know anyone." You may be by yourself, but you are related to a family. Those who are of the household of faith have more mothers, fathers, sisters, and brothers than they know what to do with who love you and want to protect you. We may not all have the same last name, but we are related and that makes us family.

Chapter Six:
Naomi: The Matriarch

Naomi's life went through seasons. She lost both her husband and sons to death and was left to carry on. Some of you have been left. You have been left by divorce or by a man who used and abused you. You have been left by the death of a spouse. You may have been left, but you have not been left alone. If you have God, you are never alone. You may have been left, but God is able to give you strength to rise up from where you are, leave where you have been, and to make it. You can have victory.

You may have been left with your ego bruised, your feelings hurt, your psyche damaged, and your image destroyed, but you are not alone. You are not abandoned because God is on your side. If God is with you, He is more than anybody else. You can raise your children, even though you have been left. You can finish school, even though you have been left. You can buy a house, even though you have been left. You can make something out of yourself, even though you have been left.

You may have been left by death and are still struggling. You can handle being left by divorce because you could say, "Well, we just didn't get along," but being left by death is final. You are probably wondering if you should feel angry with the person who left you. It is all right to feel anger, but you also need to understand there is a God of comfort who will be there when no one else is. The hurt and anger you feel is natural and normal; you should let yourself feel it, but then you have to let God heal the hurt.

You may have been left by a broken engagement, divorce, or death, but you have not been left alone. You have not been left to die. You have been left, but not by God. You have been left to succeed and prosper. You have been left to pick up the pieces and go on with your life.

THE SEASONS OF LIFE

I discovered a wonderful book years ago by Marjory Zoet Bankson entitled *The Seasons of Friendship: Naomi and Ruth as a Pattern*. Life is like a calendar and we must determine what season of life we are experiencing.

Spring is the season of "we." It is the season of nurturing and feeding, of husband and wife and children. It is the season that Naomi went through when she first married Elimelech and when Mahlon and Kilion were born. Everything was new. Spring is the season of friendship. Spring is the season of sharing your life and opening yourself up to new friends and new people.

Summer is the season of "I." It is the season when we lose our contentment and begin to wonder if there is more to life than what we have. Some people call it a mid-life crisis. You start saying things like, "Is my life over?" "Have I missed every opportunity?" "Will I ever be what I thought and dreamed I would be?" It is the season when Naomi and Elimelech left Bethlehem going to Moab. It is a season of searching.

Autumn is the season of "us." It is the season of community, family, and friends. It is a season of settling in. Elimelech and Naomi settled down in Moab. It is a season when you don't need as much.

Winter is the season of "me." It is solitude and silence. It is a season of sorrow. It is when

Elimelech, Mahlon, and Kilion died. You end up like you started out: alone.

SEASONS COME TO EVERYONE

It does not matter who you are or how much money you have, everyone is going to experience the changing of seasons.

Don't think seasons will not catch up with you. You may have the Midas touch today, but things can change. If you think, "I don't need God, I'm doing okay by myself," be careful. You do not know what the future holds, but you can know who holds the future. If you are committed to Him, it doesn't matter how the seasons change. God can give you strength to deal with every season.

Know the season you are in; every season is different and we must learn how to celebrate them. Sooner than you think the season is going to be over. The most pitiful people in the world are the ones who missed a season and are trying to recapture what is lost.

I have a friend who owns a funeral home who has observed that more people die at the change of seasons. I asked for an explanation and he said, "I don't know why, but I think it's because they've made it through one season and they just don't have the strength to gear up for another."

This makes me think of those people who have died emotionally because they don't have the strength to adapt to another change. You might be tempted to throw in the towel, but it is too early. You may have made a mess of your life, but God can help you get it back together again. Every season requires strength to adapt to it.

DON'T CHANGE YOUR NAME

The greatest problem we have is one of not knowing who we are. When we don't know who we are, we will never try to be what God wants us to be:

> *But she said to them, do not call me Naomi; call me Mara, for the Almighty has dealt very bitterly with me. I went out full and the Lord has brought me home again empty. Why do you call me Naomi since the Lord has testified against me and the Almighty has afflicted me?* (Ruth 1:20-21, NKJV)

Naomi and Ruth arrived in Bethlehem and although Naomi had been gone for years, the city gathered around her when they heard she was back. They were excited to see her and she responded with, *"Don't call me Naomi. Call me Mara."* Naomi means "pleasant and sweet" and Mara means "bitter." Why would a person change her name from pleasant and sweet to bitter?

WE CHANGE OUR NAME WHEN WE HAVE NO ONE TO BLAME BUT OURSELVES

Naomi left Bethlehem for Moab. No one put her out, no one told her to leave town and she left on her own. When she came back, her life was in shambles and she had nobody to blame but herself. What do you do when you have made a mess of your life? The first thing you do is blame somebody else. You blame your parents: "If my mother and father hadn't raised me that way..." "If my daddy had been more affectionate..." "If my mother had spent more time with me..." You blame any and everybody, but most of the problems are your own fault. The person you see in the mirror is more responsible for things that happen to you than anyone else.

The second thing you do when you mess up is to run from what you have done. If you cannot blame someone else, then you start running from your actions. You try to ignore the problem. You start making excuses for your problem. You start saying, "Nobody understands me," "Nobody cares about me," and you run from your problem. But you can only run so far and running will not solve anything. And since you are the problem, you take you wherever you go. Until you deal with what is inside you, you will never solve your problem.

You run by overeating, by sleeping all day, by getting involved in habits or activities that you know are not healthy or wholesome. That is why people drink and take drugs. It is not that it is good to or for them. Drinking and drug activity allows you to escape, and escapism takes on many forms: shopping, spending money you don't have, overeating, excessive sleeping, and so forth. In essence it is an attempt to change your name because your name is who you are. If you don't like yourself, then what do you do? You try to escape.

WE CHANGE OUR NAME WHEN WE BELIEVE LIFE HAS BEEN UNFAIR

Naomi said, *"I went out full and came back empty."* Have you ever had a moment when you felt like life had taken everything away from you? Have you ever been in a place when it seemed like life was mistreating and abusing you? You wondered why you had to suffer and everybody else was doing better than you. Life had seemingly turned on you and you could not get ahead or succeed. You wondered, "Why is this happening to me?" You have plenty of things, but you are not satisfied. You are doing the same things you have always done, but suddenly it is not fulfilling. And like Naomi you have said, "I went out full and came back empty." When you feel that life has not treated you fairly, you get mad, get even, or try to change the situation.

A lot of people are trying to change their situation by getting high, drinking, having affairs, and any number of escape tactics because life has not been fair. The reality is that life has not been fair to anybody and you are not the only one with problems. The only difference between you and another Christian is that they have learned how to take their problems to the Lord and leave them there. Everybody has problems. It is how you choose to handle problems that will determine your outcome.

Naomi chose to get bitter and it didn't work. Some of you have chosen that route, too, and it is not working for you either. You have to take your problems to the Lord and let Him work things out.

WE CHANGE OUR NAME WHEN WE THINK GOD HAS DONE US WRONG

Naomi said, "... *the Almighty has afflicted me*" (Ruth 1:20). The word used for the Almighty is the Hebrew word "El Shaddai" which means the one who can do anything. Naomi was really saying, "If God is against me, what's the use of trying?" A lot of you have given up on yourself because you have messed up. You feel that life has messed over you and God is not on your side. Don't believe that. When everybody else turns against you, God is still on your side.

Naomi said, "It is bad enough I've messed up. It is bad enough that life has messed over me. Now it looks like even the hand of God is against me." What are you going to do when life is against you and you have made a mess?

The first thing you want to do is change your name, but don't be so eager. God is not against you. He is still on your side and He is going to bring you through the trial and give you victory. The reason I know is because Ruth 1:22 says, *"So Naomi returned..."* In other words God said, "You can call yourself Mara, but I am still going to call you Naomi. You can call yourself Bitter, but I am going to call you Pleasant. You can call yourself a failure, but I am going to call you a success. It doesn't matter what you or others say, the only thing that matters is what I say."

The world may call you hopeless, but that isn't what God says. The world may say you will never make it, but that isn't what God says. God says, "I saved you, I washed you, and I redeemed you. You may have fallen, but my grace is still able to pick you up and turn you around. You may change your name, but I am still going to call you what I have always called you: My child."

It doesn't matter what you have done. You have not fallen so far that the grace, love, and hand of God cannot reach you.

Chapter Seven:
Ruth: A Study in Obedience

One thing that makes the family so valuable is that we don't have to go through a crisis alone. There is someone, somewhere who will be there for us when everything seems to be going wrong. There are people foolish enough to say, "I don't need anybody. I've got God and that's all I need," but I don't belong to that club. As long as we are in this world we are going to need somebody in our life. We were not made to live by ourselves. John Donne wrote in *Meditation XVII, Devotions upon Emergent Occasions*:

> No man is an island, entire of itself . . .
> any man's death diminishes me, because
> I am involved in mankind; and therefore
> never send to know for whom the bell
> tolls; it tolls for thee.

Family is more than just blood relatives, but includes all of the people God sends in our lives to encourage and support us. Nowhere is this better demonstrated than in the life of Ruth.

RUTH WAS A DEVOTED WOMAN

"Boaz answered and said, "I've been told all about what you have done for your mother-in-law" (Ruth 2:11). This was right after Boaz was introduced to Ruth. He had heard all about her even though she didn't know him. Her reputation preceded her. In this age of women wanting things their way and feeling they have to exert themselves, there is nothing more valuable than a woman with a good reputation. I know that sounds old fashioned, but nothing takes the place of a good reputation.

Boaz told Ruth, "I have been told about you." If that had been said of you, would you have held your breath wondering what he had heard? In this age of loose living you must guard your reputation. Ruth was a single woman with a good reputation who didn't have to worry about what Boaz had heard about her.

Boaz had heard how Ruth had treated Naomi. She loved, supported, and respected her. She was devoted to her mother-in-law.

RUTH WAS A DEVOUT WOMAN

May the Lord repay you for what you have done. May you be richly rewarded by the Lord, the God of Israel, under whose wings you have come to take refuge. (Ruth 1:12)

Ruth was from Moab, which was a land that worshiped all kinds of gods. With the influence of her husband and mother-in-law, she came to know and accept the true and living God. Ruth grew up serving other gods and married a man who was a servant of the true God. But Ruth didn't become a follower of God because of her husband or mother-in-law. At some point in her life, she learned to trust God for herself. When the going got rough and things got hard, Ruth turned to God because she knew He could help her.

When trouble comes in your life, where do you turn? What is the source of your strength? If you have not learned how to lean and depend on God, you are going to be sadly disappointed.

Timothy J. Clarke

RUTH WAS A DISCIPLINED WOMAN

"So Ruth gleaned in the field until evening. Then she threshed the barley she had gathered, and it amounted to about an ephah" (Ruth 2:17). This Scripture might not mean anything to you unless you know what gleaning is all about. Gleaning was a principle that God established as a way of taking care of the widow, the poor, and the orphan:

> *When you reap your harvest in your field, and forget a sheaf in the field, you shall not go back to get it; it shall be for the stranger, the fatherless, and the widow, that the Lord your God may bless you in all the work of your hands. (Deuteronomy 24:19)*

There is nothing sinful in needing and asking for help. It is the responsibility of the haves to help the have-nots. It is all right to need help, but you need to persevere and keep on until God blesses you, so that you can then help somebody else.

Gleaning was the biblical way of taking care of poor people. Gleaning was not a hand out, it was a helping hand. The grain was left in the field, but you had to go get it. Gleaning was not for those who

78

wanted someone to provide for them, bring it to the house, cook it, and feed it to them. It was not for lazy people.

I am sure Ruth didn't want to glean; it takes humility to go gleaning because everybody sees you. Pride is going to destroy some of you because you are too proud to acknowledge that you need help. Everybody needs help at some point, and there is no shame in honest work. As long as you are willing to work, God is willing to work with you.

THE BLESSING OF OBEDIENCE

You can always learn something new. Naomi said to Ruth, *"My daughter, should I not try to find a home for you, where you will be well provided for?"* (Ruth 3:1). It had been three months since Ruth was introduced to Boaz, and there is no doubt that when they met, sparks started flying. Ruth was a beautiful woman, and Boaz liked what he saw. No doubt they might have talked and maybe Boaz went to Naomi's house to visit. Three months have come and gone. The barley harvest is over because Boaz is now winnowing on the threshing floor. When the barley harvest ended, Boaz would be packing up and moving on.

Naomi thought to herself "They're moving too slow. Ruth is slow out of ignorance because she doesn't know what to do, and Boaz is slow because he's much older than Ruth."

Naomi decided to help them out and told Ruth, "Baby, you don't understand. Let me help you. Let me show you what to do because if you don't do something, you're going to lose Boaz." We need older people who have experience telling us what to do.

It occurred to me that as a Moabite Ruth knew nothing about the kinsman redeemer law, but Naomi did. Ruth obeyed Naomi even though the plan didn't make sense. Can you imagine what Ruth must have thought when Naomi told her what to do?

> *Is not Boaz, with whose servant girls you have been, a kinsman of ours? Tonight he will be winnowing barley on the threshing floor. Wash and perfume yourself, and put on your best clothes. Then go down to the threshing floor, but don't let him know you are there until he has finished eating and drinking. When he lies down, note the place where he is lying. Then go and uncover his*

feet and lie down. He will tell you what to do
(Ruth 3:2-4)

I guess Ruth could have thought, "Look, I've fol-lowed this woman from Moab, but she's finally lost it." But she had faith in Naomi and responded in obedience.

Imagine what might have been the outcome if Ruth had gone to one of the young women she gleaned with instead of Naomi. There is no telling what they might have told her to do. They were in the same shape she was in — gleaning in the field — so they didn't have anything either. They may have said, "What you need to do is put on the shortest, tightest dress you have. Then trick him into sleeping with you, get pregnant, and then say ah ha!" There is no telling what she might have been told if she had gone to one of the young women. Instead, she listened to Naomi and was spared unnecessary pain.

There are things I wish I had listened to, but I thought I was grown and could do what I wanted. There are things that people have been through that you don't have to experience if you would just learn to take their word for it. God's commands are not to restrict us but to keep us safe. When we obey them, we are spared hurt and pain.

Obedience positions us for God's blessings. Look at how the story ends. Ruth got what she wanted from God. Why? Because she trusted God and obeyed Naomi. It didn't make sense, but she did what Naomi said. Boaz woke up and saw Ruth lying at his feet and said, "My God, what a woman! You are so fine; you could have gone after any man. You could have had anybody you wanted, but you're not concerned only with yourself, but with your husband's memory and your mother-in-law. Since you're that kind of woman, I'm going to do what you asked me to do."

Ruth went from gleaning in the man's field to living in the man's house. She went from working with his servants to being the man's wife. She went from poverty to riches; from nothing to everything.

There is a blessing in obedience. When you trust God, He will make a way. When doors are shut and there doesn't seem to be a way, God will open up doors that no man can shut. You will benefit from the wisdom of others, you will spare yourself unnecessary hurt and pain and you will position yourself for God to bless you. God will take care of you and you don't have to lower your standards, principle, or morals.

THE POWER TO WAIT

There are some passages of Scripture that have become favorites in the sense that they are well known. Among those passages is Isaiah 40:31:

> *They that wait upon the Lord shall renew their strength. They shall mount up with wings like an eagle, they shall run and not get weary, they shall walk and not faint.*

All of us love that verse, but loving it is one thing and doing it is altogether different. Anybody can quote Isaiah 40:31, but only a few people can actually live it.

After Ruth approached Boaz about fulfilling his obligation as kinsman redeemer, Naomi told her: *"Sit still, my daughter, until thou know how the matter will fall"* (Ruth 3:18, KJV). That is a lot easier said than done.

Can you imagine what Ruth was feeling? She was a young woman who wanted to get married; her mother-in-law developed a plan for that to happen and then said, "You've done everything I told you to do. I know you're anxious and want to know if Boaz is going to do what he said. But right now all you can do is wait and see how the matter falls out." We are impatient people and we want answers now! The power to wait does not come from us; it comes from God.

There is a limit to what we can do, and when we have done all we can there is nothing else to do but wait. The world may say, "I'm the captain of my fate and the master of my soul," but there are some things you can't do. You can't change anybody. Some of you married the wrong person. The power to change people is not in your hands. The sooner we learn that, the less frustrated we will be. The most frustrated people in the world are those who have never learned or accepted their own limitations. The wisest person in the world is the one who knows he or she can't do everything.

One of the things that will help you wait is when you know you have done everything you can. Naomi told Ruth what she needed to do. Ruth followed her instructions to the letter and then Naomi said wait. She had gone to the threshing floor, had rested at Boaz's feet, pulled the covers off, and waited for him to speak. What more was there for her to do? She could not grab him by the neck and pull him to the altar! Some of you would like to use that approach, but it doesn't work.

Sometimes being right and doing right are all we have. Even when you do right, it looks like you still get messed over. Sometimes all you have is the knowledge that you did the right thing. That will give you strength when you have nothing else to show for what you have done. But before that happens make sure you have really done all you can. Have you been as loving, kind, patient, or understanding as you could be? Or, have you been standing firm and demanding your rights and your way? There comes a point when you have to ask, "What is best?" and that is not always what you want. Ruth waited because she knew she had done all she could do.

Ruth had a lot of options: Tricking Boaz, finding a younger man and forgetting about Naomi, going after her own preservation, or sleeping with Boaz and becoming a common-law wife. There was an Old Testament law that said if a Jewish man had sexual intercourse with a Gentile woman, he could not perform the act of kinsman redeemer. If Boaz had sex with Ruth, it would have rendered null and void the law of the kinsman redeemer, because you could not know the person until you were married.

She had to make a fundamental decision to do either the right thing or the expedient thing. Sometimes when you do the right thing, you don't see immediate results. You can do some things seeking instant gratification, but it won't last. You can go out in the streets and find a spouse, but they won't be anything special. Or, you can choose to do the right thing, live the right way, walk right before God, and wait on the Lord.

You can have the power to wait when it is the right thing to do. God always blesses us when we do the right thing. You may be struggling with living saved and wondering if it pays off to do the right thing. It does. There is a difference between the children of light and the children of darkness. We have been bought with a price, so we don't get to do, go, say, and act like everyone else. We are a royal priesthood and a peculiar people because Christ lives inside us.

Ruth could wait because she knew she had done the right thing and was not waiting for the results of a home pregnancy test. She was waiting on the Lord. She went to the threshing floor a virtuous woman and left the floor the same way. When you have done the right thing, you can wait.

Naomi told Ruth, "I know Boaz. He's a man of integrity and a man of his word. If he told you, 'I'm going to handle it,' then sit down. It's as good as done. We can get the invitations ready because there's going to be a wedding. I know the man we're waiting on."

If Naomi and Ruth could have that kind of faith in a human being with faults and failures, don't you think that the saints of the Lord ought to have the same confidence in the God we serve? After all, Naomi and Ruth put their trust in a man, and we are putting our trust in the God who made heaven, earth, and everything that is in it. If the word of a man is good, then the Word of God is better.

Chapter Eight:
Boaz: Forerunner of Jesus

Whenever I read Ruth 2:1: *"Now Naomi had a relative on her husband's side, from the clan of Elimelech, a man of standing, whose name was Boaz,"* the thought comes to me, "Thank God for Boaz." Why? Because he represents a prototype of what I believe every man should be striving to become. I am convinced that all men are not on drugs, in jail, beating their wives, molesting their children, or are homosexuals. God still has some real men. Men who realize that no matter what they were in the past, their lives changed once they met Jesus. I still believe that Jesus makes the difference! A drug addict before Christ now has victory. An alcoholic before Christ now has victory. A homosexual before Christ now has victory. The blood of Jesus Christ saves, delivers, and restores.

It doesn't matter what else you have going for you—money, houses, or cars—if you don't have Jesus Christ in your life, you have nothing. A man without Jesus is a failure. Sometimes we believe that if we possess material things we will be successful. Often we fail to remember that there is a difference in the success that the world gives and the success that God gives. Whatever the world gives, it can take away. If the world elevates you, it can bring you down. If the world promotes you, it can demote you. If the world makes you great, it will only last about fifteen minutes. When God blesses you, there is nothing the world can do about it.

Boaz was the kind of man who didn't run away from responsibility. That is what is destroying us as a culture and a society; we have too many men who are nothing more than what my grandmother called breath and britches. They want to look like a man, but they don't want to act like a man. You are not a man because you can drink, smoke, take drugs, or make a baby. It takes a real man to stand up to his responsibilities.

When I look at the life of Boaz, I see the kind of man I think all men should strive to be and I will tell you why: Boaz was a man of wealth, compassion, and integrity who was willing and able to handle responsibility.

BOAZ WAS A MAN OF WEALTH

Boaz wasn't a man on welfare or living from pay-check to paycheck. He was a man of means and substance. Sometimes men believe that in order to have a nice car, house, or clothes, they have to obtain it by unlawful means.

Boaz was a man of wealth, but there is more to wealth than just money. Money can buy you a bed, but it can't buy you sleep. Money can buy you food, but it can't buy you an appetite. Money can buy you a house, but it can't buy you a home. You must have something more than material posses-sions; you need a spiritual foundation.

Boaz was a man of wealth because he knew how to handle and manage money. Men need to develop the knowledge of how to make and manage money. We appear to be notorious for living beyond our means. We are forever living two paychecks ahead of homelessness. To become a man of wealth, you must learn to handle what you have now. God will not bless you with more until you learn how to handle what you already have.

Boaz knew that all wealth was not necessarily material. The Hebrew word for wealth used in Ruth

2:1 is "chayil," which not only means great material possessions, but also a mighty man of valor, one strong in strength. In other words, Boaz was not just rich with money; he was rich in his reputation, his character, and his lifestyle. There are men who are rich according to the world's standards, but they are poor in that they have no scruples or morals. There are men with lots of money who are not wealthy. There are drug pushers who could buy and sell most people, but they are not wealthy. Wealth is more than what is in your pocket; it is what is in your heart.

If you don't have a lot of money, don't feel bad because money doesn't necessarily make you rich. You can be rich in the love of your family, in the respect of your friends, and in the approval of those who know you.

BOAZ WAS A MAN OF COMPASSION

Boaz met Ruth, sent her out in the fields, and then instructed his servants to drop a few sheaves on purpose specifically for her; that is true compassion. Most men think compassion makes you weak and sets you up for someone to take advantage of you.

After all, real men are rough and tough and hard as steel. We never cry. We never express our feelings. Nothing bothers us. Personally, I don't want to be around any man who doesn't know how to cry or who is so hard that nothing breaks his heart. Being compassionate is not being effeminate.

You may be thinking, "I'm only one man. What can I do? I see the gangs, the violence, and the drugs. What can I do about it?"

> *And Jesus answering said, A certain man went down from Jerusalem to Jericho, and fell among thieves, which stripped him of his raiment, and wounded him, and departed, leaving him half dead. And by chance there came down a certain priest that way: and when he saw him, he passed by on the other side. And likewise a Levite, when he was at the place, came and looked on him, and passed by on the other side. But a certain Samaritan, as he journeyed, came where he was: and when he saw him, he had compassion on him, and went to him, and bound up his wounds, pouring in oil and wine, and set him on his own beast, and brought him to an inn, and took care of him. And on the morrow*

> *when he departed, he took out two pence, and gave them to the host, and said unto him, Take care of him; and whatsoever thou spendest more, when I come again, I will repay thee. Which now of these three, thinkest thou, was neighbour unto him that fell among the thieves? And he said, He that shewed mercy on him. Then said Jesus unto him, Go, and do thou likewise.* (Luke 10:30-37, KJV)

Let me just suggest that one man can make a difference. One man can be a big brother. One man can coach a little league team. One man can tutor for a few hours every week. One man can teach Sunday school. One man can get kids together for an educational, recreational, or social outing. You don't need a preacher's license to do some good in the Kingdom.

God has given men a certain power and authority. If you don't believe me, just think of how many times the mother asks the kids to do something and usually has to repeat the request several times; the father says it once and it's a done deal. Even if you are divorced, don't stop helping to raise your children. Your absence demands your involvement more than at any other time.

Recently the newspaper in my city ran an article about the percentage of children in our school system that come from single parent homes. While the numbers were startling and astounding, what was even more disheartening was the performance level of these children. The report showed that these children scored lower on tests, performed at lower levels in class and homework, and had more behavioral problems. Now would the presence of a father and a mother in their life solve all of that? Maybe not, but I just have to believe it would make a difference.

The Bible talks about the blessing that can only be bestowed by the father. How many of our sons and daughters have searched so many places and in so many ways for that blessing, the affirmation that only comes from a father? Brothers, if you have children, whether they live with you or not, take time with and for them. You have a place no one else can fill.

Boaz was a man of compassion because he saw a need and met it. I wish more men would do that. There is so much going on in the world today and all we need is for some men to see a need and to be willing to do something about it.

BOAZ WAS A MAN OF INTEGRITY

"I've been told all about what you have done for your mother-in-law since the death of your husband – how you left your father and mother and your homeland and came to live with a people you did not know before. May the Lord repay you for what you have done. May you be richly rewarded by the Lord, the God of Israel, under whose wings you have come to take refuge." (Ruth 2:11-12)

The preceding verses show us how Boaz related to Ruth. His actions are so different from many men today. Here was a man of wealth, position, and power. Ruth was a stranger and a foreigner, a poor widow. Boaz could have taken advantage of her. He could have said, "You hungry? I've got food. You don't have a house? I've got a house. You need some clothes? Here's my credit card." He could have said, "Baby, as fine as you are, with that body you've got, listen honey, take my whole wallet! And when they give you two keys to your apartment, just give me one and every now and then, I'll just stop by to check on you."

Boaz could have used his money to misuse Ruth, but he was a man of integrity. That is what I am praying for: Men who don't just have integrity at the church house, but at their own house. Men who don't just have integrity on Sunday, but Monday through Saturday, too. Men who are not interested in pimping the women in the Church by taking advantage of their vulnerability; playing with their emotions and affections just to massage their own egos.

One of the reasons people don't take Christians seriously is because we are holier-than-thou on Sunday and lower than dirt on Monday. The world says, "I don't understand this. How can you sing Zion's songs on Sunday and cuss like a sailor on Monday? How can you lift holy hands on Sunday and then hold a cigarette or an alcoholic beverage or play the lottery with those same hands on Monday?" If we are going to make a difference in this world, then the world must see a difference. The way we live and carry ourselves must show that we have been changed by the power of God.

A real man has integrity. A real man learns how to treat women — mother, wife, sister, daughter, and the women in the Church. Boaz was a man of integrity because he didn't try to mess over Ruth. He didn't try to play around with her.

Boaz was a man of wealth, compassion, and integrity. That is the kind of man God is looking for today. Is that the kind of man you are? Is that the kind of man you want to be? That is the kind of man Boaz was.

I will end this section by reminding you that Boaz was from Bethlehem, which is good news. If you read the entire Book of Ruth, you will discover that Boaz is the type of another man also born in Bethlehem, whose name is Jesus Christ. God used Boaz to show us what Jesus was going to be like.

THE PRICE OF REDEMPTION

Throughout this book we have been introduced to a number of traditions and unique customs that guided the nation of Israel, particularly during its infancy and early stages of development. God was shaping, making, and molding Israel into the kind of people He wanted them to be. When God lays His hand on us or calls us out, He does it so that He might transform us and make us new. God is not necessarily in the business of making us better, but different.

God gave Israel rules, regulations, and laws to govern them as His people. One of the most unusual laws was the law of the kinsman redeemer, which says that if a man died without leaving any seed, his next of kin would marry the widow, have children, and raise up the firstborn as the child of the deceased relative so the name would be carried on.

The law of the kinsman redeemer also related to property. If I lost my property through mismanagement or bad financial planning, one of my relatives could buy my property and give it back to me in my name. That is important because God wanted Israel to always own their land. All of us must learn the value of owning land. People will respect you more if you have something to call your own. You are not at the whim of everyone else when you have something that belongs to you. The law of the kinsman redeemer said that the property of Israel was never to fall into the hands of foreigners.

In the fourth chapter of Ruth, Boaz is ready to act on his role as kinsman redeemer. However, before he could do so, he had to deal with another man who was a closer blood relative. Boaz went down to the city gate — the center of Jewish culture — to find the closer relative. Old Testament cities were built with walls around them and the gate was the entrance to the city; if there was someone you wanted to see, you just waited at the gate. This was also the place where all business transactions were conducted.

Boaz *"went to the gate and sat down,"* which means that sometimes you have to wait for what you want. He waited until the nearer relative came by and then said, "Come here and let me talk to you." Boaz began talking about land and offered the man an opportunity to redeem it:

> *Naomi, who has come back from Moab, is selling the piece of land that belonged to our brother Elimelech. I thought I should bring the matter to your attention and suggest that you buy it in the presence of these seated here and in the presence of the elders of my people.*
> (Ruth 4:2-4)

The other kinsman agreed to redeem the property. Can't you see Boaz's heart drop? He is thinking, "Oh, God, I'm about to lose out here," and then he pulled out his ace in the hole: Boaz told the nearer relative that it was a package deal — Ruth and the land. Ruth was a young Moabite woman and if she outlived her husband, the land would belong to her and any children from their union. The man replied, *"Then I cannot redeem it because I might endanger my own estate. You redeem it yourself. I cannot do it"* (Ruth 4:6). Boaz had set him up beautifully.

REDEMPTION IS COSTLY

The nearer relative was not willing to pay the price for Ruth's redemption. The price he would pay was not only taking her into his home and possibly sharing his property with another man's child.

Redemption demands sacrifice. There can be no redemption unless there is someone willing to pay the price to redeem you. This is what Jesus is all about. When we were in need of redemption and no one was willing to pay the price. Jesus said, "I'll do it."

Boaz was willing to pay whatever it took to get Ruth and that is what Jesus was willing to do for us. Regardless of the price, He was willing to pay it so we might be redeemed. There is a price for redemption. For Boaz, it meant taking a risk by marrying Ruth. For Jesus, it meant giving up everything to redeem us.

Where is Ruth while all of this is going on? She is at home waiting. The law of the kinsman redeemer said you couldn't redeem yourself, someone had to act on your behalf and Boaz was doing that for Ruth. The law was clear: You couldn't buy back your own property; someone had to do it for you. You couldn't raise up seed for yourself; someone had to do it for you. You couldn't save yourself; someone had to do it for you.

That is what is wrong with the Church today. There are so many people trying to save themselves. We have so many people thinking that because they go to church and tithe that makes them saved. Money and church attendance will not save you. You need to have a relationship with Jesus Christ. It is not enough to obey the Ten Commandments, keep the Golden Rule, or go to church. Redemption is much more than that; it is what Christ does on our behalf. Redemption has a price and we can't redeem ourselves.

SOMEBODY HAS TO BE
WILLING TO PAY THE PRICE

Throughout the Book of Ruth, Boaz is representative of a type of Christ and here is why: Boaz was willing to pay the price for Ruth like Jesus was willing to pay the price for us.

BOAZ WAS A RELATIVE

A stranger couldn't redeem you, but somebody close to you could. That is what the Incarnation is about. God became man like us so we could become like Him. Somebody equal to us had to die for us. That is why the Old Testament is so full of blood because God kept giving the Israelites ways to get close to Him, but none of them fully satisfied Him. When Adam and Eve fell in the Garden, what did God do? He killed an animal, took the skin, and covered their nakedness. From Genesis to Malachi, there is nothing but blood sacrifice. This was a temporary solution because they had to keep repeating the process. God got sick of smoke, blood, and altars and sent Jesus to redeem us. Jesus wrapped Himself in humanity, came down the staircase of time, was born in a manger, lived in a ghetto, was raised in a carpenter's shop, died on Calvary, was buried in a borrowed tomb, and got up three days later with all power in His hand.

Like Boaz for Ruth, Jesus was our relative. He didn't take on the nature of angels, but He became like us so that He could identify with us.

BOAZ WAS WILLING TO PAY THE PRICE

The nearer kinsman said, "I can't do it, it will mess with my inheritance." Boaz said, "I've got my checkbook right here, and whatever it costs, I'm willing to pay." He called the elders together and said, "You are my witnesses that I have bought back everything that belongs to Elimelech. Not only have I bought back his property, but I'm also going to take Ruth to be my wife."

In his confusion one day the devil said to God, "I've been running man since the Fall, and if you want to buy him back it's going to cost you dearly." God asked, "How much do you want?" and the devil said, "It's not about how much I want, how much do you have? Whatever that is, I want it." God said, "The best I have is my own Son, and if that's

104

what it takes to redeem man, I'm willing to give Him. My Son is willing to give His life."

> *For you know that it was not with perishable things such as silver or gold that you were redeemed from the empty way of life handed down to you from your forefathers, but with the precious blood of Christ, a lamb without blemish or defect.* (1 Peter 1:18-19)

BOAZ WAS WILLING TO MARRY RUTH

It is one thing to redeem another man's property; it is another to take a man's wife. When a man marries a woman, three things happen:

- Her name changes. When I married my wife, she didn't keep her maiden name of Lawson, she took my name. When the Church joins Her husband, we will take His name, thus all believers belong to the Church of God.

- Her possessions change. When you stand in front of the preacher and profess, "With this ring, I thee wed. With all my worldly goods, I thee endow," everything the husband has belongs to the wife. Whatever Jesus has belongs to the Church. If I need healing, it belongs to Him. If I need a blessing, it belongs to Him. If I need joy, it belongs to Him. If I need peace, it belongs to Him. Whatever Jesus has becomes mine because I am His bride, a member of the Church.

- Her residence changes. When I married my wife, she moved from her parents' home into mine. When Ruth married Boaz, she moved from Naomi's house into his. I am so glad Jesus said, *"In my Father's house are many mansions"* (John 14:14). One of these days Jesus is coming back to get His bride and take us home with Him.

Jesus and Boaz were both willing to marry: Boaz to Ruth and Jesus to the Church. The New Testament calls us the Bride of Christ. When we get to heaven, there is going to be a wedding ceremony between Christ and the Church.

Chapter Nine:
Children: Our Hope for the Future

Sometimes children have a certain look in their eyes and hardness on their faces that make you wonder if there is any hope for them and their generation. The answer is yes.

We discovered that Elimelech's name meant, "My God is King." You would think a man whose parents had been good enough to name him "My God is King" would do the same for his children. Not so. Elimelech named his first-born son Mahlon which means, "Sickly and Unhealthy." God then gave him another son so he could get the naming right, but he messed up again. His second son's name, Kilion, means, "Puny and Failing." Elimelech took Sickly and Puny to live in the garbage can. Why in the world would you take someone who was weak, sick, and failing to go live in the garbage can?

This society is taking the Mahlons and Kilions of our day and forcing them to eat out of the gar-

Timothy J. Clarke

bage can. How in the world can they get strong if all we feed them is garbage? One of the biggest garbage cans we are feeding our children from is television. Television is not good or evil; it is what you do with it that determines its status. Some parents are letting their children be raised by the television. If you want peace and quiet, you tell them to go watch television. If you have a headache and want to be left alone, you tell them to go watch television. If you want to finish cooking, you tell them to go watch television. Please tell your children to go read a book! We have children who are functionally illiterate in the richest country in the world because we are letting them watch inappropriate things on television. They see people hopping in and out of bed, drugs, glamorized amoral lifestyles, and God only knows what else. Don't let your child feed on that garbage.

Don't think that just because you may not have biological children or because the ones you have are grown that you are exempt. All of us influence someone. As a Sunday school teacher, choir member, or as a Christian you influence some child, somewhere. So whatever you do, don't take them to eat out of the garbage can.

RAISING HEALTHY CHILDREN IN AN UNHEALTHY WORLD

How do you raise healthy children in an unhealthy world? God knows all that is going on in the world today, and He knows that in spite of what we see, we can raise healthy children by making sure every child has at least four things:

- Every child needs affection. What I mean is that every child needs love. You can have affection without love, but you cannot have love without affection. Every child needs to be hugged, embraced, and kissed. Some of our girls are getting pregnant out of wedlock because they grew up in homes where the father never gave them affection. Some of our boys are getting caught up in lifestyles that are destructive because they have never known true and pure affection.

- Every child needs acceptance. Every child needs to be made to feel part of something. They need a sense of belonging. Gangs are popular because they become surrogate families for those seeking acceptance.

- Every child needs affirmation. They need to be affirmed. They need to be told, "You're special. There's nobody like you in the entire world."

- Every child needs attention. Every child needs to be noticed. If you are a parent, it is wonderful to do things as a family, but you need to spend time with each of your children individually. When you do, they will not be so quick to seek what they need from someone or something else.

In addition, make sure you pray for your children, model a godly lifestyle before them, and expose them to the Word of God:

> *These commandments that I give you today are to be upon your hearts. Impress them on your children. Talk about them when you sit at home and when you walk along the road,*

when you lie down and when you get up.
(Deuteronomy 6:6-7)

Exposing our children to the Word will result in two things. First, there will not be room for anything else; and secondly, when the pressures of life squeeze, confront, and challenge them, the Word will get them through. When someone comes to them with drugs, they will say, *"My body is the temple of the Lord"* (1 Corinthians 6:19). When someone comes to them with an illegal scheme or plan, they will be reminded to, *"Present yourself holy as unto the Lord, which is your reasonable service"* (Romans 12:1).

Raising healthy children in an unhealthy world takes discipline. If you can't leave your children material things or possessions, you can leave the testimony of godly people who love the Lord. Leave them with knowledge of Jesus Christ and what He can do in the lives of people who are committed to Him. Leave them a desire to love and serve God, and we will see a change in this generation.

THE ROLE OF THE PARENTS

"So Boaz took Ruth, and she became his wife" (Ruth 4:13). The will and plan of God is for men and women to be married before they have children. Part of the problem today is that too many children are being born outside the bonds of wedlock. Boaz married Ruth. He didn't shack up with her or make an agreement of convenience with no strings or responsibility. That is the so-called modern way of doing things, not God's way.

If you have children without the benefit of marriage, God forgives, grace covers, and the blood cleanses. There is no such thing as an illegitimate child, only illegitimate relationships. Please don't think I am picking on you. My parents were never married so I know what I am talking about. I know what it's like to make up stories about why your father (or mother) isn't in the home. I know what it's like to daydream about your father (or mother). I know what it's like to wonder why your parents are not married. I pray for single parents because they have a double portion of responsibility.

I am not being judgmental, but the will and plan of God is for us to save ourselves until marriage. Then, in a healthy marriage, you bring forth children. God's plan is for children to be born within a marriage; however, that doesn't mean that everybody married should have children. Some couples are so immature and selfish that the last thing they need is to bring a child into their union. Being married doesn't automatically qualify you for parenthood.

Boaz married Ruth. That needs to be stressed. He didn't get her pregnant and leave her to bear the weight and shame of having a baby alone. If we are going to stop this systemic breakdown of the family, we have to hold people responsible when it comes to marriage. Marriage is not a game. Our spouses are real people with real feelings and emotions.

The only fighting chance our children have is to be in a home where there are loving and nurturing parents.

THE ROLE OF THE COMMUNITY

There is an African proverb that says, "It takes a whole village to raise a child." That truth is seen in Ruth 4:13-15:

So Boaz took Ruth and she became his wife. Then he went to her, and the Lord enabled her to conceive, and she gave birth to a son. The women said to Naomi: "Praise be to the Lord, who this day has not left you without a kinsman-redeemer. May he become famous throughout Israel! He will renew your life and sustain you in your old age. For your daughter-in-law, who loves you and who is better to you than seven sons, has given him birth."

The women in the community gathered around Naomi, Ruth, and Boaz. There is a community presence of support at the birth of this child.

If our children are to be saved, then the community (churches, government, schools, and neighbors) must all take part in the raising of children. We must all provide assistance, support, and encouragement to parents. If our children are going to be saved, the Church has to help by offering ministries that build up the family.

When I was a child, the entire neighborhood was my parent. I couldn't do anything wrong without somebody knowing about it and having the right to correct me. I know in today's world that would be challenging, but if we are going to save our children, we must get back to community.

THE ROLE OF THE EXTENDED FAMILY

Naomi was a grandmother with all her hopes, dreams, and desires in the child of Ruth and Boaz. Grandparents should be involved in the raising of children. Even those seniors who don't have biological grandchildren can find some child to embrace.

- Naomi took the child as her own. In other words, she owned this child. Children need to be wanted. That is why we have so many teenage girls pregnant and young boys joining gangs — they just want to feel wanted.

- Naomi laid the child in her lap, which means she loved him. Children need love. If you can't give them money, the latest designer outfit, and the newest gadget, you can give them love. That will do more for them than anything else.

- Naomi became the child's nurse. The Hebrew word for nurse is "awman," which means to build up and support, to turn to the right; to teach, instruct, guide, and counsel.

Naomi did more than just nurse him in the typical sense. She also became the baby's teacher. Our children need teachers. If you are going to be a teacher, you must lead by example. We must teach them by what we say, what we do, and how we live.

Is there any hope for our children? It is in your hands. The only hope for our children is parents who love the Lord, a caring and loving community to provide support, and an extended family that will nurture, guide, and instruct. None of that happens without Jesus Christ in our life. The only true hope is Jesus. When we let Him in, He will make all the difference.

Conclusion:
Don't Give Up!

Throughout this book we have discovered a lot about Naomi and Ruth. We have read of their highs and lows, mountains and valleys, and have learned so many lessons from them about life, love, commitment, and family. There is one more lesson they can teach us about handling what life brings our way.

The one consistent theme about the life of Naomi and Ruth is that they never gave up. A lot of bad things happened to them and a lot of things came their way that may well have made them want to give up, but they had a tenacity and perseverance not often found in our world today. They teach us the lesson of never giving up.

We all need to learn the art of not giving up. No one said that life would be easy, that everybody was going to like us and that we would never have a problem. You are not going to get through life without problems, disappointments, setbacks, and pain. But you must make up your mind that no matter what happens, by the grace of God you are not giving up.

I heard a story once of a general who was interviewed after a victory. The interviewer asked, "Were your men braver, stronger, and smarter?" and the general replied, "My men were braver, stronger, and smarter five minutes longer!" In other words, if they had given up five minutes earlier, they would have lost.

You may be about to let go of the rope, walk out on a relationship, or give up on God, but hold on five more minutes. Help is on the way.

Naomi and Ruth teach us to never give up and that when you think it's over, it's only just beginning.

NAOMI AND RUTH TEACH US
TO NEVER GIVE UP ON GOD

"Blessed be the Lord who has not left you without a kinsman redeemer" (Ruth 4:14). You might be wondering what this is all about, so I will tell you. These women are telling Naomi that what happened in her life was a direct result of the work of God. Even

when we don't see Him, God is always at work. There are a lot of people who pray and never see results. They think, "Well, there's no use in praying, nothing's going to change." Listen, you must remember that just because you don't see God working doesn't mean He is idle. God is working when we least expect it.

I am sure there were times when Naomi and Ruth wanted to give up on God. There are times you and I want to give up on God, too. When that happens, we cannot let the devil sell us a bill of good. *"Praise be to the Lord, who has not left you. . ."* is the heart of the Book of Ruth. Through it all—the good and bad; the highs and lows, the mountains and valleys—God never left them. And He won't leave you either.

God is faithful and always keeps His Word. Whatever He has promised will come to pass; and when you cannot hold onto anything else, you can hold onto Him.

Timothy J. Clarke

NAOMI AND RUTH TEACH US
TO NEVER GIVE UP ON OURSELVES

The women told Naomi that the child would be *"a restorer in your old age, a blessing to you"* (Ruth 4:15). They were saying that the child would give her back some of the years she thought she had lost. I am sure there were times when Naomi and Ruth felt that life had passed them by and it was all over. The baby brought a new lease on life.

You still believe in God, but you are ready to give up on yourself. You had a child out of wedlock and you think that is the end of your life. You fell into sin and you think that is the end of your life. You got tangled up with drugs or alcohol and you think that is the end of your life. Naomi and Ruth are reminding you "Don't give up on yourself."

I cannot imagine where I would be if I had given up on myself. I am not exactly a prime candidate for success. I was not voted most likely to succeed at anything, but I met a Man who said, "If you stick with me, I'll take you places and do things in your life that you never thought possible." I took Him at His Word and gave Him my life, and He has done everything He promised and more. When the world gave up on me, and even when I was ready to give up on myself, there was a God who never gave up.

NAOMI AND RUTH TEACH US
TO NEVER GIVE UP ON OUR CHILDREN

Now these are the generations of Pharez: Pharez begat Hezron, and Hezron begat Ram, and Ram begat Amminadab, and Amminadab begat Nahshon, and Nahshon begat Salmon, and Salmon begat Boaz, and Boaz begat Obed, and Obed begat Jesse, and Jesse begat David.

The above genealogy from Ruth 4:18-22 (KJV) is one of the most important parts of the Book of Ruth. Genealogies are normally pretty boring, but this one ties David into the tribe of Judah. Naomi probably looked at Obed and thought, "Well, I don't know. His father is considerably older than his mother. The neighbors know his background and people can be mean when they know your business. I don't know if he's going to amount to much." She didn't know that while she was holding Obed she was holding

David's grandfather, and that David would become the greatest king Israel would ever have.

Naomi also didn't know that coming from David was another King — the king of Kings and lord of Lords. Watch how you treat the children around you because you don't know what they will become. Don't give up on the children. They may not look like much now, but there is no telling what they will become.

I was born prematurely and the doctors didn't think I would survive. I wasn't much to look at, but I came into this world fighting. When I was a teenager people told me I wasn't going to amount to much because I was from the wrong side of the tracks and had the wrong family tree. And for a long time I believed them and I stopped taking school seriously because I thought, what's the use in trying since I'm not going to amount to anything? And then one day I heard a preacher say, "God can take your life out of the muck and mire and make something beautiful out of it." That had a profound effect on me and I responded to the call and told God, "I really do want to be something. I want to be somebody," but all the voices in my ear said, "Nobody and nothing; nothing and nobody." I told God, "I really want to be somebody" and He said, "If you trust me, I will make you somebody." And He did. I don't mind telling people every chance I get where He brought me from. What He has done for me, He will do for you if you give Him a chance.

God hasn't given up on the family and neither should we. With God's help, the family can become all that God intends. Let's start *Celebrating the Family*—both biological and spiritual—and watch God work.

Please enjoy this excerpt from
Living in the Blessed Place, ISBN 978-0-9764022-8-2

There is a place in God where we move beyond a blessing to living a blessed life. It doesn't matter how old you are, how much in debt you are, or how many bad decisions you have made. If you have faith to believe that God is able to reverse your situation, then you, too, can start living the blessed life in the blessed place.

The blessed place is not reserved for super saints or those who have been pure all their lives. The blessed place is for people who live in the real world with real problems. We serve a God who is able to turn our mess into miracles. You may think it can't be that simple or easy, but it is. God has the power and He is no respecter of person, but He is a respecter of faith. And wherever God sees faith, He steps in, moves, and performs a miracle.

We don't like to talk about living in the blessed place because a few preachers have misused, misquoted, and misrepresented this teaching. We have stayed away from it lest we become lumped in with them. That is a trick of the devil. Just because some people abuse the teaching doesn't stop it from being true. When we fail to preach it, and then fail to live it, we deny the saints a powerful part of their inheritance as sons and daughters of God. The Bible says, *"My people are destroyed from a lack of knowledge"* (Hosea 4:6).

It is not the will of God for His people to be ignorant. We have not taught the saints the fullness of their inheritance. Saints have died never experiencing the fullness of life that God, through Jesus Christ, by the Holy Spirit, says they can have. We have put them in a spiritual straightjacket. Jesus came to give us life and that more abundantly. Enjoy your salvation. It is God's will to bless us, and when we don't walk in those blessings we live short of God's best for us.

Some years ago I heard a story of what might happen to us when we get to heaven. According to the story, God will show us all the things that could have and should have been ours; yet, we never believed nor asked for them. Now I know that story is not a biblical truth, but it helps to point out how far below our potential we often live.

Perhaps because of our background we tend to think that if we ask God for too much, we will bankrupt Him and heaven. We will never out-dream or out-do God in His abundance, His provision, and His desire to bless us. What God told Abram is what He says to us, "I will give you as far as you can see," and God sees us *Living in the Blessed Place!*

Other Books by
Bishop Timothy J. Clarke

Caution! God at Work – Trusting God through tough times

Celebrating the Family: Lessons from the Book of Ruth

Living in the Blessed Place

Making the Most of Your Time

The Price of Victory: Strategies for winning a faith fight

Reclaim Your Spiritual Health

To My Sisters Beloved: A trilogy of encouragement